# VEGAS 2UZ3

# Carol Moore

*Vegas Travel Guide*

*Vegas Travel Guide*

# Table of Contents

*Vegas Travel Guide*

# Introduction

One of the most well-known towns in the country, Las Vegas, is known for its exhilarating entertainment, magnificent casinos, and opulent hotels. Las Vegas, which was established in 1905, has expanded to become the biggest city in Nevada and the heart of the world's entertainment industry. The history, society, and landmarks of Las Vegas are covered in this introduction.

In 1905, a group of trained employees established Las Vegas. The area at the time served primarily as a rest point for tourists and refugees making their way to California. But in 1931, Nevada authorized gaming, making Las Vegas a popular tourist location. Since then, Las Vegas has developed into the top tourist spot in the world for gaming and amusement, welcoming more than 42 million visitors annually.

Some of the most famous places on earth are located in the metropolis. Las Vegas is well known for its opulent lodgings, top-notch cuisine, and exhilarating entertainment. Numerous casinos, such as the Bellagio, MGM Grand, and Caesars Palace, are also located in the city. Among the noteworthy occasions that take place in Las Vegas are the World Series of Poker, the National Finals Rodeo, and the Consumer Electronics Show.

Furthermore, Las Vegas is well known for its way of life. The Nevada State Museum, the Las Vegas Art Museum, and the Las Vegas Natural History Museum are just a few of the numerous galleries and institutions that make up the thriving city's art scene. Las Vegas also offers a huge selection of eateries, nightclubs, and gambling establishments. Numerous live music places can be found throughout the city, including the well-known Las Vegas Strip.

As a result, one of the most well-known towns in the country is Las Vegas, which is famous for its thrilling amusement, magnificent casinos, and opulent hotels. The city has expanded into the biggest in Nevada and the center of the global entertainment industry. Las Vegas is a location that should not be overlooked by anyone seeking a memorable experience because of its variety of sights, events, and culture.

# Map of Vegas

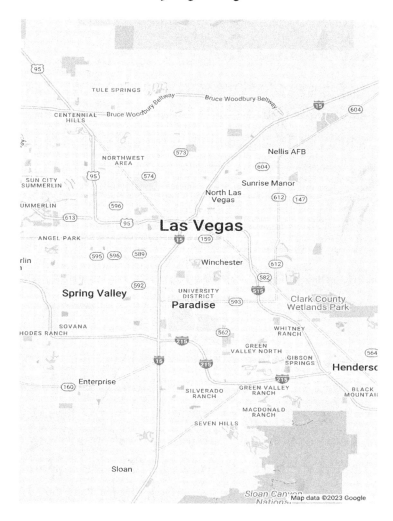

# Chapter One

## Accommodations

Vegas is one of the world's most famous tourist locations. With its dazzling lights, world-class casinos, and lively entertainment, it's no surprise that people flock to the city for a weekend escape. When it comes to lodging, however, Vegas has an abundance of choices for tourists, spanning from low-cost hotels to opulent casinos. There are numerous lodging options in Vegas, whether you want a low-cost alternative or a lavish encounter.

There are numerous cheap lodgings and dorms for those on a tight budget. The Circus Circus, the Flamingo, and the Excalibur are among the more famous options. These motels, which are often situated in the center of Vegas, provide essential conveniences such as televisions, Internet access, and air conditioning.

For visitors seeking an opulent experience, the Las Vegas region has several costly motels and eateries. Some of the most famous options for those looking for a pricey hotel are The Bellagio, The Venetian, and The Wynn. These hotels and resorts provide a variety of facilities, including saunas, exercise centers, and swimming areas, in addition to exquisite eating and amusement.

Many motels provide easy rooms and amenities for guests with special requirements. The Las Vegas Convention Center offers a wide range of services and facilities, as well as unique suites for people with physical impairments and other special requirements. There are also wheelchair-accessible paths and special needs accommodations at the Luxor.

Overall, based on your requirements and price, there are numerous lodging options in Vegas. From opulent casinos to low-cost motels, Las Vegas has accommodations for every income.

*Vegas Travel Guide*

You can be certain that among its many choices, you will find the ideal lodging to meet your requirements.

## Hotels

The hotel ambiance in Vegas, one of the most luxurious cities in the world, is no exception. From luxurious five-star hotels to cheap cottages, Vegas has something for everyone. Saunas, concierge services, and specialty stores are among the lavish amenities found in deluxe hotels in Las Vegas. The Bellagio Hotel and Casino, which looks out over the world-famous Las Vegas Strip, is one of many of these hotels with spectacular vistas of the city. Vegas has a variety of low-cost accommodation choices, including the Travelodge Las Vegas, which has typical amenities like a pool and a fitness center.

Vegas has a broad range of lodgings, so whatever you're looking for can be located there. There are numerous luxurious accommodation choices in Las Vegas, including the well-known Caesars Palace and the famous Bellagio. These hotels offer a variety of amenities, ranging from luxurious lodgings and flats to ostentatious recreational services. High-end hotels in Las Vegas are known for their dedicated workers and excellent customer service. For those who prefer a more relaxed atmosphere, there are numerous mid-priced accommodation options. In addition to a relaxing atmosphere, these lodgings frequently include standard amenities such as a pool and a fitness facility.

For tourists seeking a genuine Vegas experience, there are numerous accommodation options. Well-known hotels such as the Venetian and the Palazzo offer a more traditional Vegas experience, complete with music, gaming, and other activities.

Furthermore, these accommodations offer a variety of dining and entertainment options. For those looking for a more modern environment, there are many specialized hotels in Las Vegas. These hotels are frequently more private and have sleek, contemporary designs.

Whatever your budget or tastes, Vegas has something for you. Vegas has a broad range of accommodation options, from luxurious five-star hotels to low-cost cottages. Whatever type of encounter you seek, Vegas has it, from the famous Caesars Palace to the iconic Bellagio. There are motels in Vegas to fit all preferences, whether you want an opulent getaway or a more laid-back holiday.

## Resorts

Las Vegas, Nevada, is well-known for its lavish hotels, showy casinos, and thrilling entertainment. However, beyond the dazzling lights and commotion of the street, Vegas is home to a plethora of casinos that offer a diverse variety of services, amusement choices, and accommodations for visitors of all kinds. A property in Vegas can suit every taste and budget, from luxurious five-star hotels to cheap flats.

For those seeking a luxurious experience, the Bellagio, MGM Grand, and Venetian are some of the most well-known casinos in Vegas. These sites offer first-rate amenities such as spas, fine dining, and entertainment. For a more affordable option, Excalibur and Luxor Resorts offer comfortable accommodations, a variety of delicious restaurants, and an abundance of exciting entertainment options.

Numerous casinos in Las Vegas provide modern amenities and services for business visitors. The Four Seasons, Mandarin Oriental, and Wynn Las Vegas are among the finest luxury business hotels in the region, offering cutting-edge conference amenities, meeting places, and business services. For those searching for a more inexpensive option, the Stratosphere Hotel and Casino, the Renaissance Las Vegas Hotel, and the SLS Las Vegas all offer a plethora of business amenities and services.

For tourists who want to experience the local natural scenery, many casinos in Vegas offer breathtaking views of the desert and mountains. The Red Rock Casino Resort and Spa is a popular option for those seeking a more relaxed, outdoor experience. For those looking for a luxurious leisure experience, the Green Valley Ranch Resort and Leisure, which offers a variety of treatments, saunas, and pools, is an excellent option.

No matter what kind of experience tourists are looking for, there are many casinos in Vegas offering a variety of services and activities.

A property in Vegas can suit every taste and budget, from luxurious five-star hotels to cheap flats. Because of its diverse array of attractions, events, and accommodations, Las Vegas is an excellent destination for tourists of all kinds.

## Vacation Rentals

Las Vegas holiday accommodations have grown in appeal as a popular alternative to hotel lodgings for visitors in recent years. Vacation lodgings in Las Vegas range from extravagant palaces to inviting condos and provide a unique and often more inexpensive way to experience the city. Because of its extensive assortment of sites, entertainment, and activities, Las Vegas is an ideal location for a vacation home.

When booking a vacation rental in Las Vegas, there are a few important things to consider. The hiring number should be prioritized. Smaller condos may be preferable for couples or lone travelers, whereas bigger homes may be suitable for large groups. Second, do your research on the property and the area to ensure that they satisfy the group's criteria. Third, double-check the rental agreement to ensure that all fees, payments, and taxes have been taken into account. Finally, tourists should invest some time perusing reviews made by previous visitors to get a real feel of the property's quality.

Las Vegas holiday houses have numerous spectacular features. These could include a fully working kitchen that allows guests to save money on eating out, as well as a private pool or Jacuzzi for an extremely luxurious stay. Many lodgings also include a variety of entertainment facilities, such as large-screen TVs, computer terminals, and outdoor activities. Some lodgings may include access to nearby attractions such as golf courses, gambling, or entertainment areas.

The cost of vacation lodgings in Las Vegas can vary greatly depending on the size, location, and characteristics of the facility. The price is usually set per night, with discounts possible for longer stays. Taxes and other additional costs may apply, so read the rental agreement carefully before making an appointment.

In conclusion, Las Vegas vacation cabins are an excellent alternative to traditional accommodation. Holidaymakers can make the most of their stay by researching the property, its amenities, and the surrounding area. Given the diversity of sizes, locations, and prices, there is likely to be a property that suits the needs of any gathering.

# Chapter Two

## Attractions

Las Vegas is one of the world's most popular tourist destinations, renowned for its thrilling nightlife, spectacular shows, and diverse range of activities. This flourishing desert city has something for everyone, from the famous Las Vegas Strip and Bellagio to the globally renowned Las Vegas Zoo and Aquarium. From the numerous performances and acts to the thrilling casinos and entertainment parks, Vegas has a lot to offer.

The Las Vegas Strip is the city's most recognized feature. The Bellagio, Mandalay Bay, and Venetian are just a few of the well-known and luxurious hotels and casinos that line this four-mile stretch of Las Vegas Boulevard. Visitors can enjoy a wide range of entertainment options, from world-class shows to expensive eating and shopping.

The Bellagio is one of the most recognized landmarks on the Las Vegas Strip. This historic hotel and resort's magnificent water show is accompanied by classical music and lights. The Bellagio also has an excellent art museum, a prestigious gym, and a variety of expensive shops and restaurants.

The Las Vegas Zoo and Aquarium is a popular attraction in the city. This magnificent zoo contains over 200 various species of animals, including lions, giraffes, rhinos, and others. Visitors can also view the aquarium's entertaining exhibits, which feature a variety of marine creatures.

The Adventuredome, the world's largest subterranean theme park, is one of many amusement parks in Las Vegas. This five-acre park features thrilling roller coasters, exciting activities, and other attractions. Visitors can also enjoy a go-kart track, a water area, and the Las Vegas Mini Grand Prix.

*Vegas Travel Guide*

Finally, any journey to Las Vegas should include a stop at the Fremont Street Experience. This public square features live music, dazzling lights, and a variety of street performers. Visitors can also participate in a variety of activities such as zip-lining, light shows, and more.

The renowned Las Vegas Strip, the Bellagio, the Las Vegas Zoo and Aquarium, and the Fremont Street Experience are just a few of the attractions in Vegas. Vegas has a broad range of encounters to fit every visitor's tastes.

# Shows

Las Vegas is a top entertainment destination with a diverse range of shows for visitors to enjoy. There's something for everyone, from energetic Cirque du Soleil performances to classic Penn & Teller comedy. The Blue Man Group and Cirque du Soleil's The Beatles LOVE, two of the world's biggest theatrical shows, both appear in the metropolis. Numerous smaller-scale shows provide their audiences with a more intimate experience.

Las Vegas has an incredible variety of shows, ranging from plays and stand-up comedy to magic acts, acrobatic routines, and more. These programs are split into two main categories: production shows and resident performances. the of and a, and a, and a, and a, and a, and a. These initiatives typically have a brief run, generally a few weeks.

Resident performances, on the other hand, are long-running bands that frequently stay in the city for months or even years.

# Map of Bellagio Hotel

# Casinos

Las Vegas is one of the most well-known and well-known cities in the globe. It is famous for its casinos, entertainment parks, and bars. Since the city's inception in the early twentieth century, casinos have played an important part in the Las Vegas experience. Casinos have long been a staple of the Las Vegas experience, from the ostentatious and extravagant Strip casinos to the more familiar and down-to-earth downtown venues.

The casinos in Las Vegas attract a wide range of participants, from high rollers to those looking to have a good time. The main attraction in Vegas is gaming, and due to the massive variety of games, everyone can find a game that suits both their interests and their budget. While table games such as blackjack and roulette provide a more focused and strategy-based experience, slots, and video poker are popular choices for those seeking a more laidback and low-stakes experience.

*Vegas Travel Guide*

The atmosphere of the casinos in Las Vegas is one of their major attractions. From the dazzling lights and buzzing energy of the main gambling rooms to the more private and homely settings of the clubs and bars, there is something for every type of gambler. Furthermore, casinos offer a variety of amenities such as fine dining, live entertainment, spas, and haircuts. This means that even if you don't want to participate, you can still enjoy the casino's atmosphere.

Casinos in Las Vegas are great locations to gamble, but they also offer a variety of other activities. While many casinos have poker rooms where you can fight against other players, others have bookies where you can bet on sporting events. Live performances and comedy performers are another popular attraction at many casinos.

Las Vegas casinos have come a long way since they first debuted in the early twentieth century.

They now offer a broad range of encounters, from extravagant and flashy Strip casinos to cozier and more modest city locations. Whatever your interests are, Vegas is sure to have something for you.

## Museums and Cultural Centers

Las Vegas has long been associated with opulence and entertainment. However, the city is also home to a large number of museums and cultural organizations, allowing visitors to learn more about the region's past and culture. Visitors can visit a variety of fascinating groups, including the Neon Museum and the Mob Museum.

The Neon Museum is a well-known landmark in Las Vegas. The museum, located in downtown Las Vegas, is dedicated to preserving the city's famous neon signs.

Visitors can view the museum's exterior exhibit, which features more than 150 restored antique signs from Las Vegas. There is also an internal display with a variety of odd artifacts and signs at the museum.

The Mob Museum is another popular attraction in Las Vegas. The display, located in the center of Las Vegas, is dedicated to documenting the past of organized crime in the United States. Through interesting exhibits, visitors to the museum can learn about the history of the mob and its impact on American culture. The museum also contains a variety of artifacts, such as firearms and other items associated with organized crime.

The Las Vegas Natural History Museum is another notable attraction in the area. The museum, located on the Las Vegas Strip, is dedicated to educating visitors about the natural world.

The museum features some interesting exhibits that explore the history of the area's flora and animals. The museum also houses a large collection of artifacts and other objects that cast light on the region's historical history.

The Las Vegas Art Museum is another creative establishment in the city. The museum, located in downtown Las Vegas, is dedicated to exhibiting a wide range of artwork from around the world. The museum holds some recurrent exhibitions that feature works by a range of artists. The museum also maintains a permanent collection of works in various creative forms such as painting, sculpture, and photography.

There are also numerous smaller creative organizations in Las Vegas. The Nevada State Museum, for example, is dedicated to educating visitors about the state's history. The museum has many continuing exhibits that explore the region's past, from its early inhabitants to the present.

*Vegas Travel Guide*

The museum also has a library and a theater, which are used for a variety of events such as lectures and workshops.

Las Vegas has a plethora of museums and cultural organizations. The city's monuments allow visitors to learn more about the region's past and culture. Visitors can visit several fascinating organizations, including the Neon Museum and the Mob Museum.

## Outdoor Activities

Outdoor activities in Las Vegas are a great way to see the city while moving and getting some fresh air. From hiking in the nearby Red Rock Canyon to kayaking down the Colorado River, there is something for everyone. Hiking is one of the most popular recreational activities in Las Vegas. The Red Rock Canyon National Conservation Area is an excellent destination for hikers of all skill levels.

With its granite structures, canyons, and wealth of creatures, it is an incredibly beautiful spot to explore. There are numerous pathways for both novice and expert hikers, ranging from casual strolls to rigorous treks. Kayaking is another popular recreational activity in Las Vegas. The Colorado River runs through the city, providing a beautiful backdrop for an afternoon of kayaking. Visitors can appreciate the scenery while learning about the region's history and flora and wildlife on one of the many guided kayak trips available.

In addition to hiking and kayaking, Las Vegas has a variety of other outdoor activities. Mountain biking allows you to see the stunning scenery of Red Rock Canyon. There are numerous biking routes for riders of all skill levels, ranging from easy roads for beginners to challenging routes for specialists.

*Vegas Travel Guide*

Camping is another popular activity in Las Vegas. There are both municipal and private campsites available, ranging from primitive to fully-equipped RV parks. Numerous rivers in the area also offer great opportunities for swimming and fishing.

Families will enjoy the outdoor activities available in Las Vegas. The Springs Preserve, with its pathways, flora, and animal exhibits, is an ideal location for a family outing. The Wet 'n' Wild Las Vegas Water Park, with its slides, pools, and winding rivers, is a great place to cool off in the summer. The Adventure Dome at Circus Circus is also a great location for family fun, thanks to its internal amusement park activities and distractions.

Outdoor activities in Las Vegas are a great way to see the city while moving and getting some fresh air. Visitors of all ages and abilities can enjoy activities ranging from hikes in Red Rock Canyon to kayaking down the Colorado River. Las Vegas has something for everyone, whether they want a relaxing vacation or an adrenaline rush.

# *Chapter Three*

## Dining

Las Vegas has an unrivaled eating experience. The city has eating choices for every type of client, from casual spots to fine dining locations. From renowned chefs to hidden gems, Las Vegas has a broad range of culinary delights to offer. Whatever your taste or budget, you can discover something to pique your interest.

For those looking for a more traditional dining experience, Las Vegas has a broad range of costly restaurants. Whether you favor French, Italian, or American cuisine, you can find it here. Famous chefs such as Gordon Ramsay, Wolfgang Puck, and Bobby Flay have all opened restaurants in Las Vegas.

For a more intimate meeting, you should visit one of the city's many hidden gems. These places frequently provide a unique eating experience at a fraction of the cost of more well-known spots. They are frequently concealed away in alleyways or at the back of casinos.

For those looking for a more relaxed atmosphere, Las Vegas has a variety of options. Everything from athletic organizations to family-friendly restaurants is available. Many of the city's casinos have restaurants serving a wide range of cuisines, including classic American meals and cuisines from other nations. In addition, there are numerous fast-food restaurants and food vendors in the metropolis.

Las Vegas has a flourishing nightlife scene. There are live music venues, cafés, taverns, and gatherings, so there is something for everyone on a night out. Whether you want a peaceful evening out or an all-night party, you can find something to do.

*Vegas Travel Guide*

Whatever food or location you favor, Las Vegas has something to satisfy your appetite. From the most expensive restaurants to the most laidback cafés, you can find something to titillate your taste buds anywhere. You can find cuisine to suit your flavor, from well-known chefs to unknown gems. You can also find something to keep your night going in locations ranging from bars and gatherings to live music venues. Las Vegas has an unrivaled eating experience.

## Restaurants

The variety of restaurants in Las Vegas is well recognized. The city has a wide range of eateries to suit every flavor, from elegant dining to quick cuisine. From the fabled feasts at the Bellagio and the world-famous burgers at In-N-Out Burger to the unique fusion cuisine at Osteria Costa and the traditional Italian food at Rao's, it's easy to see why Las Vegas is a popular vacation destination for foodies. Whatever your taste, Las Vegas is sure to have something to satisfy it, whether you want a quick bite or a fine-dining experience.

When it comes to fine food, Las Vegas is home to some of the world's most well-known restaurants. There is something for everyone, from Joel Robuchon's classic French cuisine at the MGM Grand to Charlie Palmer Steak at the Four Seasons. Other expensive eateries in the area include the Michelin-starred Restaurant Guy Savoy at Caesars Palace and the Estiatorio Milos at the Cosmopolitan, which offers modern Italian cuisine.

For those looking for a more relaxed dining experience, Las Vegas has a lot to offer. From conventional American burgers and milkshakes at Shake Shack at the New York-New York to Mexican street food at El Dorado Cantina at the Mirage, there is something for everyone. Other popular quick food restaurants include Buca di Beppo at the

Venetian and VegeNation at Downtown Container Park, which serves vegan-friendly dishes.

In Las Vegas, you can find a wide variety of international cuisines. There's something for everyone, from classic sushi at Sushi Roku in the Forum Shops to unique flavors at Tamarind in the MGM Grand. Other international eateries on the Gold Coast include Ping Pang Pong, Cleo at the SLS Hotel, Galbi at the MGM Grand, and Galbi's Korean BBQ at the MGM Grand.

Whatever food you favor, Las Vegas is sure to have something to satisfy your appetite. The city has something for everyone, whether you want a quick bite or a formal dining experience. Las Vegas, with its diverse dining options, is an ideal place to explore the world of food.

# Bars and Nightlife

Vegas is well-known for its exciting nightclubs and flourishing nightlife. This city has something for everyone, from renowned clubs to hidden speakeasies. For those looking to have a wild night out, there are numerous bars to choose from, varying in price from the ultra-exclusive to the more affordable. For those looking for something a little more low-key, some many bars and clubs offer a private atmosphere with specialty beverages and live music. However, Vegas has every type of amusement experience imaginable.

The city is home to some of the world's most well-known nightclubs, including XS Las Vegas, Marquee Las Vegas, and Hakkasan Las Vegas. The world's biggest celebrities and VIPs visit these mega-clubs, which feature some of the best DJs and live acts. These clubs have a lively atmosphere with dazzling light shows and the latest party music.

Make sure to dress appropriately before entering because many of these locations require uniforms.

For those looking for something a little more low-key, there are numerous eateries and bars to choose from. From craft breweries to opulent hotel eateries, there is something for everyone. The city also has a flourishing craft cocktail culture, with many places specializing in both conventional and cutting-edge drinks. Because they frequently feature live music, these establishments are ideal for relaxing with friends.

There is something for everyone in Vegas when it comes to amusement. There are numerous places to go, varying from luxurious clubs to homey cafés. Whether you want a wild night out or a more relaxed atmosphere, Vegas will not disappoint. Take a glass, then let the twilight wash over you.

# Chapter Four

## Shopping

Shopping in Las Vegas is an unforgettable experience. The city is well-known for its abundance of shops, depots, and companies offering an almost infinite variety of goods. There is something for everyone in Las Vegas, which provides both high-end names and fairly cost products. You can buy anything in expensive retail stores and lavish shops. Furthermore, many of the shops and depots are walkable, so you don't even need to leave the city to shop.

The Las Vegas Strip is home to some of the world's most well-known shopping centers. The mile-long Miracle Mile businesses at Planet Hollywood feature over 200 businesses and restaurants. Designer labels such as Gucci, Prada, and Michael Kors are offered.

The Fashion Show Mall is another well-known shopping location with expensive stores and a variety of restaurants.

If you're looking for something a little different, go to Downtown Container Park. This outdoor shopping location is home to charming shops, regional art galleries, and food vendors. The Grand Canal Shoppes at the Venetian Resort are another must-see for luxury shopping. High-end shops such as Chanel and Versace, as well as a variety of restaurants, can be located here.

For those looking for lower prices, Las Vegas also has several storage and production facilities. The Las Vegas North Premium Outlets, which offers more than 150 stores at discounted prices, is one of the city's most popular shopping destinations. The Las Vegas South Premium Outlets is another well-known outlet-buying complex that offers a wide range of apparel and products.

Purchasing in Las Vegas is an unforgettable event. The city's numerous shops, marketplaces, and companies make it straightforward to find whatever you require. There is something for everyone in Las Vegas, which provides both high-end names and fairly cost products.

## Malls

Although Las Vegas, Nevada is well known for its vibrant nightlife and plethora of entertainment options, the city is also home to some of the world's most spectacular casinos. The Grand Canal Shoppes at The Venetian and Palazzo are massive, and the Forum Shops at Caesars Palace are opulent. Las Vegas locations offer a diverse variety of luxury dining, entertainment, and shopping choices.

Whether you're looking for premium apparel and accessories, one-of-a-kind presents, or simply want

*Vegas Travel Guide*

to browse and sight-buy, the city's shops have something for everyone.

The Forum Shops at Caesars Palace is one of the most well-known retail locations in Las Vegas. The Forum Shops, situated in the heart of the Las Vegas Strip, offer a true luxury shopping experience. The building houses over 160 premium stores, including Gucci, Prada, Versace, Louis Vuitton, and Cartier. In addition to the upscale stores, the complex has a wide range of eateries, including those operated by renowned cooks. Live music performances and live shows are just two of the options for entertainment at Forum Shops.

The Grand Canal Shoppes at The Venetian and Palazzo are another well-known retail complex in Las Vegas. The mall, located in the heart of the Strip, offers a unique shopping experience with its Italian-inspired architecture and canals.
The building contains over 170 shops, including high-end merchants such as Burberry and Salvatore

Ferragamo. In addition to the upscale stores, the mall has a variety of eateries ranging from formal dining establishments to quick food places. The complex also offers a range of entertainment options, such as watercraft excursions and live music performances.

There is also the Boulevard Mall in Las Vegas. The Boulevard Mall, located in the city's southeast, offers a wide range of mid-priced and low-cost stores, as well as several dining and entertainment options. The building contains over 150 stores, including those offering clothing, jewelry, and domestic goods. In addition to the shops, the complex has several restaurants, a theatre, and a bowling alley.

Las Vegas has some of the most remarkable cities in the world, with a wide range of dining, shopping, and entertainment options.
From the opulent opulence of Caesars Palace's Forum Shops to The Venetian and Palazzo's

massive Grand Canal Shoppes, Las Vegas has something for everyone. Whether you're looking for premium apparel and items, one-of-a-kind presents, or simply want to browse and the city's shops provide a truly luxurious shopping experience.

## Markets

Las Vegas is a vibrant city renowned for its extensive gaming area and thrilling nightlife. The city's markets play an important part in its business by offering a diverse variety of goods and services to locals and tourists alike. Las Vegas has a diverse market, ranging from packed public bazaars to luxury shopping malls. Whether you're looking for souvenirs, apparel, or fresh cuisine, Las Vegas has something for everyone.

The Fremont Street Experience is a popular mall in Las Vegas. This five-block outdoor square in the city's heart is home to a variety of stores,

*Vegas Travel Guide*

restaurants, and street entertainers. During the day, you can purchase anything, including clothing, jewelry, kitschy presents, and handcrafted jewelry. At night, the square comes alive with light shows and live music.

The Premium Outlets at Las Vegas is another well-known emporium in Las Vegas. This upscale bargain center has over 140 stores, including brands like Prada, Gucci, and Coach. Even if you don't want to purchase anything, the mall's vibrant atmosphere and colorful stores make it an enjoyable place to pass the day.

For those looking for a more traditional market experience, the Las Vegas Farmer's Market is an excellent option. On Saturdays, this open market offers a range of fresh produce and handcrafted goods. There are also food booths serving delicious regional cuisine and live music at the market.

Last but not least is the Las Vegas Flea Market. A massive outdoor market with hundreds of vendors takes place at the Cashman Center. Everything from antique furniture to vintage clothing is offered here. The market is an excellent place to find unique items at cheap prices.

You're sure to find whatever you're looking for at one of Las Vegas' many markets. From high-end shopping malls to outdoor bazaars, Las Vegas has something for everyone.

## Boutiques

Vegas is well-known for its expensive stores that offer high-end name clothing, accessories, and makeup. Although there are many locations to purchase in Las Vegas, these stores provide a unique shopping experience for both visitors and locals. Boutique shopping caters to all tastes, from the opulence of the Bellagio to the more subdued elegance of the Wynn.

If you want to buy at expensive shops, head to the Strip. Many of the most well-known fashion brands, including Balmain, Gucci, and Dolce & Gabbana, have stores in the city. Customers can buy items that are truly one-of-a-kind from these exclusive stores because they are not available anywhere else. Because of the opulent displays and dedicated employees, these stores are locations in and of themselves.

For those looking for a more relaxed shopping experience, the Las Vegas South Premium Outlets offer a broad variety of premium goods at reduced prices. This complex's more than 130 stores sell renowned brands such as Coach, Michael Kors, and Juicy Couture. The mall is a great place to spend the entire day because it has a diversity of eating and entertainment options.

Along with larger shops and companies, the city is home to a large number of smaller merchants. These stores offer a variety of items, including handmade items, jewelry, vintage clothing, and accessories. These stores provide customers with a unique shopping experience and frequently stock items that are not available in larger stores.

When it comes to purchasing in Vegas, there is something for everyone. You can find anything in Vegas, whether you want costly premium products or less expensive options. Because of the abundance of stores in Vegas, it is perfect for a high-end shopping trip.

# Chapter Five

## Transportation

Las Vegas, known as the "Entertainment Capital of the World," has a transportation system that can handle its many visitors. From the well-known Las Vegas Strip to its vast desert landscape, the city offers a variety of methods to get around. The Las Vegas transportation system consists of buses, vans, taxis, cars, trains, and ride-sharing services.

The Regional Transit Commission of Southern Nevada (RTC) is in charge of ensuring the safe and efficient running of public transit in the Las Vegas urban area. The RTC operates the Deuce and the Strip & Downtown Express, which are the two major bus routes that transport commuters to the Strip and downtown. The Strip & Downtown Express runs between the major casinos and hotels, while the Deuce runs the entire length of the Strip. The RTC also operates many transportation routes to connect passengers to and from the airport, the city core, and the Strip.

Las Vegas provides a variety of taxi and transit services for visitors' comfort. Taxis and limousines offer convenient door-to-door service and are easy to hail on the street or book through a local provider. For longer trips, the Las Vegas Monorail is another great option. A seven-mile stretch of the Strip served by the train system connects the bars and casinos to downtown Las Vegas.

The growth of ride-sharing services such as Uber and Lyft has made it easier than ever to get around Las Vegas. Users of these services can use their mobile devices to order conveyance and pay for it through the program. Using ride-sharing services, visitors can quickly and cheaply explore the metropolis.

Other means of transportation in Las Vegas include electric scooters, motorbikes, and even airplanes. Visitors can explore the region by renting bicycles or using the city's many motorized bike services. Visitors can hire a private plane for a more personalized experience, or they can take a chopper flight of the Strip for a more luxurious experience.

Overall, Las Vegas has a well-developed public transportation infrastructure that can accommodate the city's large number of visitors. There are numerous modes of transportation available in the metropolis, including buses, cabs, limos, railroads, and ride-sharing services. With so many transportation options, Las Vegas is sure to provide visitors with an enjoyable and useful way to explore the city.

# Conclusion

Las Vegas, Nevada, has grown to be a well-known travel and gaming destination. There is a lot more to Vegas than first appears, despite the perception that it is a sanctuary of opulence and entertainment. Numerous schools, museums, and other cultural attractions are located in the metropolis. However, it is crucial to take the societal and cognitive repercussions of the city's culture into account when making conclusions about Vegas.

Las Vegas is renowned for its excess and opulence. People visit Las Vegas in search of entertainment and enjoyment, and it is common for tourists and gamblers to develop an addiction to the joys of the gaming tables. In addition, the city is home to many alluring attractions like casinos,

*Vegas Travel Guide*

concerts, and amusement that can cause obsession. Overconsumption can have disastrous financial consequences, mental illness, and other negative effects.

The environment in Las Vegas has the potential to psychologically foster the development of poor behaviors. Gambling and depression, anxiety, and even death have all been linked. People may become fixated on trying to achieve despite the consequences because the thrill of success can be addictive. A casual approach toward sex and alcohol can also lead to risky behaviors with long-term effects.

For people who struggle with mental regulation, Las Vegas can be a dangerous place. It is challenging to resist the environment's many diversions, and it is simple to succumb to the city's sights, sounds, and culture. People are easily influenced by those around them, making it difficult to make rational decisions in such circumstances.

*Vegas Travel Guide*

To sum up, Las Vegas is a lavish city where it is easy to get caught up in the excitement of the moment. Although the city can be entertaining and enjoyable, it is important to take the social, psychological, and neurological effects of the city's culture into account. While in Vegas, visitors should be aware of the risks and keep control of their decisions.

Printed in Great Britain
by Amazon

22678013R00036